BUSINESS TRANSFORMATION
The Roberts Story

BUSINESS TRANSFORMATION
The Roberts Story

By Jim Hull with Brad Hart

Cover layout and book design by
Christopher Green Design
christophergreen.com

Printed in the United States of America
10 9 8 7 6 5 4 3 2 1

FIRST WORDS

"The purpose of the word is to convey ideas; When the ideas are grasped the words are forgotten"

- Chang Tzu

"Your transformational strategy must match the customer's needs and contain value that creates a competitive advantage in order to deliver a sustainable profit"

-Jim Hull

"He who builds the best Supply Chain wins"

- Brad Hart

FOREWORD

This book is a story in the form of an interview with Brad Hart, the CEO of Roberts Tool Company. It presents the essence of his company's transformation. Initially the transformation plan was based on four operational elements. These were the elimination of set up (preparation) time, utilization of equipment, employee development and stable processes. Success on the first two elements required customer cooperation. To achieve this objective a new work flow pathway had to be created from the customer to Roberts. Herein lay the strategic secret to success. Roberts found a way to connect with the customer strategically and create a flow of the "right work" in the right quantities. This allowed for the implementation of a cell strategy. The cells were created to add a value and profit solution to the flow of work obtained under the new working relationship with the customers. So, unlike most companies that build cells and then set about to "fill them up", Roberts found the work first. Only then did they build a cell to deliver on customer price points and Roberts' profit objectives. This approach of obtaining the work before investing in equipment and processes is the last part of the secret to the success of the transformational process. Creating a continual flow of the right work, and the right production solution, is the one and only way to solve the on time delivery issue on a sustainable basis. It was a process that began with the input of customer understanding and commitment. The output of the process resulted in the integration of customer price and organizational profit. This successful output was a result of the recognition that a sustainable flow of the right work was a prerequisite for success.

Lean, six sigma and other operational excellence programs helped along the way. They were used to support the continuous improvement effort. The catalyst in the process, however, was a successful strategic sales and marketing program.

Marketing activities allowed Roberts to collect all of the information in relation to customer needs and expectations. Sales provided the proposals to those needs. It was this marketing and sales activity that created the glue that held the transformation process together. You will learn more about this process in the pages that follow. So while this is not a book on lean, six sigma or continuous improvement models, these ideas were used to help fashion a successful transformation. We thank the many authors who have written books on these subjects. They have helped us to better understand how to use these tools. We also thank our peers and colleagues without whose feedback we would never have arrived at the ideas that we put forth in this book. And last, but not least, we thank Kellie Gaskins and Ellie Hull for their support and ideas both of which contributed significantly to the final product.

Brad Hart and Jim Hull
Los Angeles, California USA

Contents

INTRODUCTION

The customer sets the price! You set your profit objectives. As an organization your customer solutions must meet both of these criteria and are thus created to deliver on both customer price and your profit. To embrace this integrated concept of customer price and organizational profit is to enter into a new world of opportunity and success. While most organizations fight customer requests, or demands for price reductions, the successful ones will embrace this reality and work to achieve it. In fact, the real competitive advantage will go to the organization that develops and proposes cost cuts before the customer can ask. This is the Holy Grail!

The Customer Value Proposition, which consists of product, customer support, price and innovation, is one of several of the key elements of an aerospace organization's business model. Today the customer value proposition is focused on price. Products and customer service, in the form of on time delivery, 100% quality, and information transparency, have become expectations and not matters of differentiation. They are the 'table stakes'. Today's world class organization realizes that delivery on price is critical in order to meet or exceed the expected value to the customer. It is the way that the organization contributes to the customer's ability to compete.

How is this achieved? Those who willingly, or grudgingly, agree to price reductions without any changes to their business model will fail. This is because if productivity is not improved then all price reductions come at the expense of profit. So the question becomes how does one improve productivity? Operational excellence, and the innovation that it suggests, is a solution to improvement in the area of productivity. Lean is an example of an Operational Excellence approach that focuses on increasing speed of throughput (Sales) through the removal of process and organizational waste. As an organization wide management approach, it provides a way of achieving the commensurate levels of productivity necessary to allow for the customer's price reduction needs without loss of profit. It is a win – win equation and not a zero sum game. It is the productivity approach that Roberts chose to pursue in its transformational process.

As the chosen way for improving productivity Roberts had to address the reason why lean failed to deliver on its promise to so many organizations? They found it was because of the traditional point of view held by suppliers. Most suppliers have not seen it as a way to deliver on their customer value proposition thus making their customers more competitive. Instead they saw lean as a way for the customer to impose ever more stringent requirements on their suppliers. As a result of this misunderstanding, many supplier organizations have failed to achieve the promises of lean and other operational excellence approaches. Most have tried to apply parts of lean which result in a lot of unsustainable activity and confusion. A typical approach is to first apply the organizational and 'clean up' tactics known as 6S to their operations. This work refers to the steps of sorting, setting (placing), shining, standard (for cleanliness), sustaining and safety. It is the business equivalent of keeping your "room picked up and clean" and having a proper place for everything. If that step is successful then most organizations move onto individual operational process improvement events known as Kaizen Events. These events are developed to improve a specific area of operation using lean ideas and approaches. Usually some progress is gained in a specific area but at a great expense of time and effort. Most organizations then tend to regress, and in some cases lose all of the time and money invested in these two steps. Most organizations have not realized that lean, or other continuous improvement program tools, cannot succeed on their own. They must be integrated with other transformational components. In the case of Roberts Transformational Model these additional components were sales / marketing, cells and talent development. This omission occurs for most organizations because they have not taken the time to work through the most important step in the transformational processes. This is the PREPARATION STEP.

The Preparation step, as created by Roberts, consisted of the following four elements.

Cultural Change

As a supplier organization it is your purpose to make your customers more competitive. An understanding of this idea must be embraced by all employees. How and why it is the way that they are going to approach work in the future must not only be accepted by all employees, but welcomed as a new way for them to succeed. It is not a project, but rather a total transformation of the organization to a better and more effective way of doing business. This understanding at the employee level is the primary key to the sustainability of organizational transformation.

Process Stability and Standard Work

This refers to process documentation, development and performing a process/ task the same way each time. This is based on an organization's current understanding of the current 'best practice' or best way for each task to be accomplished. This is a specific part of the cultural understanding that makes continuous improvement possible. All employees must enthusiastically embrace this element.

Daily Follow Up and Reinforcement

Taken in the form of Gemba or Gemba Walks (An intentional form of 'Management by Walking Around'), this is a portion of management work. The purpose of the Gemba Walk is to check on such things as process adherence/ changes, standard work compliance/ changes, quality and production schedule attainment. Other Visual Management Strategies can be used to insure the communication of objectives, values and performance measures. In addition, performance based compensation plans and other rewards for exceptional performance can be developed and implemented.

Roberts Transformational Process

Roberts integrated four process elements to make up the Roberts Transformational Model (RTM). These are in the form of processes. They are lean, marketing and sales, cells, and human asset development. Lean, as our primary continuous improvement tool, embodies those process improvement projects that will allow us to achieve operational excellence and become more productive. The marketing and sales processes allow us to work with our customers strategically to develop work that fits our capabilities (or work to develop new capabilities that the customer needs). The cell processes allow us to create a lean solution for the selected work that can deliver on our customer value proposition. The human asset development process insures that we select, develop and reward our employees in order to continually improve our portfolio of human assets. These four processes, that make up our RTM, consistently generate better outcomes for Roberts' customers. These allow Roberts to be the low risk, low cost supplier that the customers need in order to compete successfully.

Preparation is the basis for any successful and sustainable transformation. Until these preparatory steps have been achieved, and it may take a year or more, it is a waste of time and money to embark on any ad hoc operational improvement programs. Preparation is the foundation and making customers more competitive is the objective.

So the moral of the transformation story to follow is:

- Low Cost/ Low Risk - To compete customers and their suppliers must reduce the price it costs to deliver quality products on time.

- Improving the capability to deliver solutions in the form of Cells, or other manufacturing models, allow suppliers to become more productive leading to the profitable reduction of prices to customers.

- Continuous Improvement, based on industry requirements, is a proven method to permanently improve operational performance and allow the organization to be more competitive. It will help in delivering on the product and customer service portion of the customer value proposition.

- Selecting the best work through strategic customer marketing and sales efforts along with continuous improvement and cells is the way to create a sustainable transformation.

- Culture change, talent development and continual improvement in the value of the human asset portfolio provide the human energy needed to successfully transform and sustain progress.

Leading with a low risk/ low price focused transformational strategy is the portal to the development of a competitive advantage. This book is about Roberts' transformation and the stories behind it. These are shared in the hope that they will help other supplier organizations become more competitive. Today Roberts' organization, and its customers, successfully competes world-wide on price, product, customer service and innovation. You are invited to do the same.

PART ONE

TRANSFORMATION PREPARATION

CHAPTER ONE
ELEVEN BELIEFS AND SIX LESSONS

1

*What is the first
consideration
for any plan to
transform an
organization?*

The customer sets the price. If you believe this you have to admit that what you are doing currently is probably not going to create the results that you and your customers need for the future. More of the same will not get you where you need to be in order to continue to compete and generate profits. This means that you have to change what you believe. If you cannot, or will not change what you believe, you will not have any room for new ideas. So the first thing you have to do is to release yourself from your old ideas and open up to a new potential set of beliefs. During the preparatory stage, and as you create your new set of beliefs, you will begin to experiment. These will lead to new lessons learned and you will begin to set yourself up for the creation of your transformation process. You will create new stories for yourself and your organization.

These are the beliefs and lessons that we have learned. They have helped us to achieve success with the transformation of our organization. The stories that are provided throughout the book depict actual situations that occurred along the way. They describe the challenges and new solutions that we were able to develop once we adopted a new and more effective point of view represented by our RTM. These innovative developments were the result of our focus on the objective of making our customers more competitive. We begin with a Leadership story which is where all successful transformations must embark.

Brad's Leaders Commitment Story

Our journey began 10 years ago. It began with a financial commitment requiring a cut in pay for all three owners. We did this as we recognized the need to transform our company. While our customers had not yet arrived at the point where they would require our transformation, we could see this need arising. Like all insights it was not comfortable at first. We did not even initially trust that we knew what the future held. In the end we decided that the expected rewards outweighed the costs and proceeded. Our first step was to seek outside advice. This outside advice came in the form of a lean expert. He brought new knowledge and a more effective way for us to see our business. In reality he taught us to SEE the possibility for our business. He did this by helping us to create a new point of view. He trained us on Lean principles, created a Kaizen Newspaper, and led us to the development of our first real cell. This latter achievement led to the acceptance of the 'cell concept' as our way to deliver on the manufacturing portion of our solutions. We then realized that the idea of a cell was a process solution to many issues in our business. This was to influence our future beyond our initial expectations. What we did not realize, however, was the amount of time and effort it would take to actually change the culture. Naively we believed that all we had to do was to train the employees and they would naturally embrace the ideas of lean and cells. Were we wrong! Even our best employees had a difficult time embracing the need to change. Once we turned our back their tendency was to default back to their old ways. We then learned the importance of daily Gemba Walks (MBWA – Management by walking around) to maintain conformance to the new processes. But like a lot of other companies on the lean journey, we found it difficult to sustain our progress. Our tendency was to develop pockets of change and excellence amid the old culture. We had, however, begun our journey and were committed to seeing it through. This is the first test of an organization's resolve. Leadership must commit and follow through on those commitments if the employees are to follow.

Leadership must be based on a new belief system.   These are the beliefs that we have developed on our journey. Remember you have to let go of your old beliefs in order to make room for the new ones!

OUR ELEVEN BELIEFS ABOUT TRANSFORMATION

These beliefs allow us to make our customers more competitive.

1. **Customers:** To be effective a supplier organization must seek, and obtain customer understanding and cooperation at the strategic as well as operational levels.

2. **Purchase Order (PO) System:** To succeed any transformation requires a process whereby an organization can obtain a flow of the 'right work'. Today a successful supplier organization will connect with the customer procurement process in a unique way in order to capture product families, instead of individual parts, where cost savings can be realized. The organization will be working with customers to identify needs, and allocate dedicated capacity. This process, and its success, will dictate the potential performance of all of the other processes.

3. **Manufacturing Environment:** The closer an organization can come to a 'product'

manufacturing environment, as opposed to a 'job shop' environment, the closer they can come to consistently fulfilling all aspects of a customer value proposition.

4. **Branding, Marketing and Sales:** An organization needs to have a core competency in these areas to be successful with any transformation. Branding, or how you are perceived by your customers, prepares them to choose you at the "moment of selection". Marketing deals with uncovering customer needs and opportunities. It is the portal to "finding the right things" to work on. Sales, as distinct from marketing, are those activities associated with developing customer relationships and maintaining a flow of the right kind of work.

5. **Transformational Thinking:** Today's supplier organization must have a visually based thought process whereby they can think in the transformational terms of observation, rapid learning and prototyping, and collaboration in

order to create innovative/ cost effective solutions for their customers.

6. **Financial Modeling:** Today an organization needs to have a core skill in financial modeling of customer solutions. An ability to see the solution mathematically allows the organization to make the right decisions in constructing and developing a solution.

7. **Human Asset Development/ Employees:** Transformational thinking and culture change requires training, development, accountability and recognition systems for all employees. It is a given and not an elective. Most employees are marginally qualified and thus the organization is not getting the maximum benefit from these assets. It must be understood that the employees are the most valuable asset. Any expense incurred in their development is an investment and not a cost. Recognition for exceptional performance is a must. Today's organization offers careers and not just jobs to attract and keep the best talent.

8. **Information/ Transparency:** A traditional supplier organization does not provide enough information to the shop floor or the customer. In order to make the customer more competitive the lean supplier must have a transparent production process where the customer and production employees have real time access to all necessary information. In addition, innovative analytics provide a new way for the supplier and customer to compete. Here analytics refers to the innovative use of data and analysis to drive decision making. It is the way you understand and use your business data to make more informed decisions.

9. **Management:** An effective management team that can continually improve, innovate and run the operational aspects of the organization without the daily involvement of the owner is a requirement. In most cases this will require coaching, training and/ or upgrading of personnel.

10. **External Collaboration and Supply Chains:** Supply chain development,

management and continual improvement, have traditionally been the weakest part of a traditional aerospace business model. To begin to work on it is like moving from a game of checkers to one of three dimensional chess. While this level of collaboration may be difficult to create and maintain, it is always worth the effort. It is a strategy that creates an impermeable barrier to competition for the supplier and the customer.

11. **Processes** - A supplier organization cannot succeed without stable processes. This must be accomplished before embarking on the development of cells or any other higher level manufacturing strategy. Once stabilized they need to be under a continuous improvement program.

Continuing on from our beliefs the following lessons are what we have learned as we experimented and why WITHOUT THESE LESSONS most transformations have failed. This Story on Culture is a lesson that leads the way.

Brad's Culture Story

Once you have developed a new set of beliefs you can begin to change the culture. This is perhaps the most important part of the preparation for any company. A culture indoctrinated into transformational thinking and based on a new set of beliefs, must precede any successful transformation. Our old culture had several missing elements that needed to be developed. In our case the most important one was our lack of focus on the development and success of our work force. While we were never abusive, we had a blind spot when it came to employee recognition and development. Our expectation was that our employees were hired to do a job and that was what we expected them to do. This led to a culture of fault finding, finger pointing and criticism. We were quick to blame, but not to thank or appreciate. This type of culture would never be successful in absorbing the level of change that we were expecting. We began to visualize a new approach. Our first prototype initiative was to develop a performance based compensation program. We decided that we needed to show the employees that we were serious about recognizing them for exceptional effort. While this program alone did not change the culture, it showed the employees that the leadership of the firm was committed to material change. It resulted in a changed relationship with our employees and was the doorway that allowed us to move forward with our culture development process. Today our employees are making their own commitments to excellence. This would never have happened if we had not taken this first move.

As we changed our beliefs we began to learn new things. We opened ourselves up to seeing things in a way that allowed us to learn new lessons.

THE SIX LESSONS THAT WE HAVE LEARNED ALONG THE WAY

1. **The Business Model Lesson** – A transformed organization will have a business model that reflects a Customer Value Proposition that meets all current core customer needs. It is dynamic and therefore requires knowledge of the transformational model and processes. It changes as the customer's needs change. This ability of the Leader to create successful and adaptable business models is the first lesson to be learned. Today a company may go through a number of changes in their business model in a single generation of 30 to 50 years. Without the knowledge and ability to change and transform business models, the owner, and the management team, cannot cope with these demands.

2. **The Productivity Lesson** – 'Doing more with less' is the motto of any disciplined organizations where sales can increase without an incremental increase in employee cost. This lesson suggests that additional productivity is gained from working with each individual employee. Improvement in processes and the application of new technologies also make the customer more competitive. It is a partnership between management and the company's employees to deliver ever increasing customer competitiveness.

3. **The Leader's Business Point of View Lesson** – The traditional organizations business point of view is internally focused on making products and delivering services. The transformational point of view suggests a marketing and sales approach. This leads to creating solutions through stable processes and tools in order to make the customer more competitive. This lesson tells us that the

traditional leaders' (Owners and Managers) point of view does not fit most transformational models. This point of view needs to be changed if any transformation is to be achieved.

4. **The Profitable Competitive Advantage Lesson** – Any transformation should deliver more value to the customer and more profit to the organization through the development of a new and more competitive business model. This lesson shows that the purpose of transformation is to provide a way to help the customers become more competitive; while not jeopardizing supplier profitability.

5. **The Leader's Lesson** – The development of the leader's standard work is a critical part of the new business model. The leader's standard work is that group of regular activities that the leader does each day, week month and year to lead the organization in its on going transformation. It is always a work in

progress. Here the lesson is that without the leader's standard work, successful company transformation as an on going activity will never be realized.

6. **The Continual Improvement (CI) Lesson**
In a transformed supplier organization improvement never stops and all business processes need to be under CI. You cannot implement a CI program until the business culture has embraced and follows the processes and standard work methods for producing products and services.

Brad's Continuous Improvement Story

We called the part to be manufactured the Beehive. That metaphor seemed to best fit the look of this complex manifold. This was one of our first attempts to apply lean pricing principles and exemplifies how we have become more competitive. Our customer had set a target price. Knowing that the 'customer sets the price' we accepted the target price as a given. We went to work to develop a manufacturing solution that could meet that price and also our profit goal. The historical method for manufacturing this manifold took ten hours of set up time. As a result of our new method and cell process, we reduced the set up time to zero hours and reduced the price by 20% thus exceeding our customer expectations. We accomplished this with collaboration. We used a team approach to engineering, planning and development of the manufacturing process. The centerpiece of our solution was our cell strategy. In the end we made our profit goal and our customer's expectations were exceeded. We learned that creating a cell based on specific customer requirements is the key to meeting or exceeding our customer's expectations.

These SIX LESSONS and the preceding ELEVEN BELIEFS prepared a mental framework within which culture change could be achieved. These are the key structural elements that were developed, understood and accepted by all leaders within our organization. Once this was accomplished, as a part of the leader's preparation, the transformational work with the rest of the organization began.

Remember that first you must make room for new beliefs and subsequent lessons by setting aside the old way of thinking. Before you can change the way you do work you must first change your way of seeing and believing. Failure will follow if this advice is not heeded. And it is not just a change, but a passionate change of mind and beliefs that is necessary. Emotion and passion need to be present to provide resilience in the face of the hurdles that you will encounter. Transformational journeys are the most difficult ones that any leader has to face. It is the unknown that has to be penetrated and you must have passion in order to have the courage to do so.

Chapter Two, a case study, will provide a preview as to the transformation that can result in increased customer competitiveness and organization profit.

CHAPTER SUMMARY AND KEY TAKE-AWAY POINTS

- A passionate leadership commitment is required for any successful transformation.

- The leader must have the enthusiastic support of the management team to assist in leading any transformation.

- An organization must first prepare before embarking on a transformational journey.

- For any transformation to be successful an organization's culture must change, first by setting aside old beliefs and then adopting a new set of beliefs.

- An organization must have a dynamic business model based and a constantly updated Customer Value Proposition.

- A new way of thinking in transformational terms is critical in order to envision and create a new business model.

- In today's environment the customer sets the price and the organization must be able to deliver on it in order to meet or beat the competition.

- RTM, represented by the four part integrated strategic matrix, is the way Roberts created and structured their business transformation.

Brad's Last Word

"Transformation stems from leadership and the leader must grow and change before the company has a chance to move to the next level."

CHAPTER TWO
A LEAN STRATEGY EXAMPLE

2

*If I embark on a
transformational
journey, and am
successful,
what kind of
operational and
financial results
can I expect?*

Since the customer is setting the price you must have all of the elements of your model working so that you can consistently predict and perform to the customers' desired level. Your transformational journey is an investment that you are making in time and resources to create a more effective future. The following is a hypothetical example based on our real experience.

A cell is a lean manufacturing process that has been designed to reduce waste and improve speed.

This includes the physical elements of machinery, human resources and processes. This example describes the application of this concept as a way of winning new work while maintaining or increasing organizational profitability.

The Opportunity

The supplier organization has established a process where the customer has sent 'families' of parts instead of individual parts for quotation. Further, the organization and the customer discussed the ideal product model that fit with the supplier organization's competencies. In this way the customer pre-selects specific families of parts thus saving time and waste in the traditional quote process. In this case the customer has asked for a competitive quote on a family of pre-selected parts. In order to reduce their risk this customer is placing larger packages of work with fewer qualified suppliers.

Assumptions

1. A family of 20 parts

2. The organization must be able to deliver one set of 20 parts a day

3. The target price must not exceed an average of $150 @ part. (Note: the current average price per part for this family from the current suppliers (several) is $167.00. Therefore they are seeking a 10% reduction in price.

4. The original cost to the supplier was $150.30 per part. This means that they had a 10% profit which would go away once they accepted the price that was now required by the customer.

The Lean Assessment

The family of parts is the 'right kind of work' and it is from a preferred customer.

The Solution:

The following is a typical lean solution (Build a cell for the manufacture of the 20 parts) for this type of customer opportunity.

Here is an example of how a cell can be financially modeled to achieve these results. As you build the model you focus on developing your cell to meet customer needs but not exceed them in terms of value that cannot be recaptured in the form of revenue. Equipment that is too robust, or finishes on parts that are not required, do not create a lean cell environment. The goal is not to over build or over produce with the process. The process should meet but not exceed requirements.

Modeling the Solution

Cell Design Assumptions

1. Annual Sales – $1M

2. Number of Parts – 20

3. Work Day – 20 hours

4. Yearly Work Hours – 5,000

5. Annual number of parts required at 80% capacity equals 4,000

6. Required Takt Time (Pace of production)– 1 part per hour

7. Projected Takt Time from Assumptions – 1.25 parts per hour

8. Projected Cell Capacity Load at required Takt Time = .80

9. Complete PQ Analysis (Product Quantity Analysis/ Four Part Process/ Forecasting Model.

10. Create Basic Cell Process to Cost/ Profit ($150 per part)

The Cell Cost Model

Design the Basic Cell Process

1. 1 Lathe/ 1 mill

2. Set up Time = 0

3. Run Time average (for 1 part) = 60 minutes

4. 1 person running two machines – 2 shifts + lead

    a. Labor = $400 a day/ Two employees @ $20 @ hr. in two shifts

    b. Material = $150 a day

    c. Equipment = $190 a day/ Average payment on two Machines at $200,000 per machine

    d. Utilities = $50 a day

    e. Total Daily Direct Cost = $790 a day

    f. Indirect (Burden) = $160 a day/ Incremental cost of sales (note: This is not necessary if you are adding to existing production where all of the burden costs are already being covered by other work centers – or you can lower the burden rate/ allocation to all work centers to reflect the new income stream)

    g. Total Daily Cost = $950 a day

    h. Total Daily Throughput = (20 parts)($150) = $3,000

i. Maximum Daily Profit/ Contribution
= $2050 a day(68% Profit)

In the past these 20 parts were quoted and produced separately. By packaging them as a family of parts the customer has made it possible for the supplier to develop a more productive solution. Further it allows the customer to become more competitive while at the same time making the supplier profitable.

As a process, the key is to 'front-end load' the organization with the right work. Next you proceed with the target pricing and develop a cellular solution that will meet the target and yield the maximum organizational profit. The process must also perform in the areas of on time delivery and quality. This requires that the organization invest more time on the front end planning stages so that a long term and sustainable solution can be fashioned for the customer. The result is that you become the LOWEST RISK/ LOW COST SUPPLIER. You are making your customer more competitive while maintaining your company's health through profitable production. The customer asked that the price be reduced but the organization's ability to create a cell has also improved the quality (one piece flow) and drastically reduced the lead time.

While we slightly exaggerated the performance in this model we did so to get your attention. It shows, in simple terms, the potential once you begin to think differently about your organization's transformation. We also use this new way of thinking to reengineer old jobs. This is a process that we have set up to insure that we are improving new and repeat jobs for our customers.

The next chapter will provide an introduction to the marketing and sales process that is responsible for creating a flow of the right work from the right customers.

CHAPTER SUMMARY AND KEY TAKE-AWAY POINTS

- First assume that the customer sets the price!

- To keep a customer competitive you need to create a solution that meets or beats the target or market price while delivering on time and to the required quality standards.

- You create a solution process by looking for ways to reduce the asset (resources including time) requirements.

- Start with the price and work backwards into the process requirements to deliver at or below that price.

- Consider 'reframing' the solution many times.

- Create prototype solutions and integrate new lean concepts.

- Select the best solution and implement.

Brad's Last Word

"He who acts and fails is closer to the solution than he who only complains."

PART 2

THE STORY OF THE ROBERTS
TRANSFORMATION MODEL

CHAPTER THREE
SALES AND MARKETING EXCELLENCE

3

*What approach
should a
supplier
organization
take to create a
successful
marketing and
sales strategy
and operation?*

Even though the customer sets the price most
organizations still begin their journey inside their
organization with a focus on operational excellence.
An organization, however, cannot maximize its
profits and business value on operational excellence
alone. While operational excellence is important, it
is not enough to carry the day. Warren Buffet, the
well known business investor, has stated this many

times and in many different ways. His opinion, which has led him in his investment methodology, is that an organization must have a "franchise" of some form in order to have high sustainable profits. It must have something unique that many people want and can only get from one, or a limited number of sources. In his opinion operational excellence is not powerful enough, on its own, but must be married with some unique capability. So while operational excellence cannot stand as a singular solution, it is still necessary to be at the top of that game in order to provide a sustainable production platform and culture.

Focusing on sales and marketing excellence instead of operational excellence is where our Roberts Transformational Model begins to depart from the traditional approach. Initially, like many others, we started our transformation with a traditional approach focused on operational excellence. We discovered that it did not work on a sustainable basis. Even as we were approaching vast improvements on operational process improvement we were not able to sustain a good on time record with our customers. We knew that there must be a reason and solution but would not have guessed that we would find it in the marketing and sales area. In fact, from our perspective we were very good at marketing and sales.

Roberts' focus had always been on developing customers and increasing sales. Further we had the President and two employees working full time on the customer side of the equation. Who could have asked for a better commitment to marketing and sales? We had done such a good job that at one point we had buried our engineering and planning area with over 140 new jobs. We did this in spite of our core customer's anger over our lack of on time delivery.

Working with our strategic consultant we decided to explore the cause and the remedies. Initially we started by listening to our own engineering and planning department. They had been trying to tell us what we needed to do for some time. We had not paid attention to them. They told us that we only had the capacity to plan a certain number of new jobs each month. Their ability, and that of the shop floor and the quality department, to produce and ship on time was greatly governed by the amount and type of work we brought in from the customers.

What did that mean? Did it mean that we had to stop marketing and servicing our customers? While we did not argue with them we felt that it was just a part of the 'game'. It was the way the industry worked and you had to take on whatever jobs your customer needed.

From a marketing and sales perspective you had to be the 'go to' supplier. That was our attitude. This time, however, instead of ignoring our staff we decided that we needed to investigate further. How could we solve this problem on a sustainable basis?

First we decided that we had better give ourselves a chance to catch up. We formed a New Job Review Group. This was made up of a representative of engineering, production, quality, sales and marketing. The goal was to review all of the new potential work once a week and decide which 'one' new job to add to the backlog.

Secondly we decided we needed to take a hard look at how we were working with our customers. What we discovered was that we had fallen into the trap of assuming that we did not have control over the process.

We had assumed that we had to work within the bounds of the way that the industry operated. We were wrong!

The key was not to try to be the best within the process but rather to change the process. It was not that we were not as good as others in dealing with the current procurement process but rather that the bid and placement process was flawed. It was missing a key element that was to change our direction and make our transformation possible.

This element involved approaching our marketing and sales work with a strategic instead of tactical methodology. Our company relationships had always been at the buyer level where the day to day work of RFQ's and PO's take place. We had never spent time developing our relationships and solutions at the strategic buying level. It had never been on our radar screen.

As so often happens when you make such a discovery things start to operate to assist you in your plans. A former buyer of one of our biggest customers approached us with a business employment proposition. His former employer was one of the ones angry with us because of our lack of on time delivery.

As you would expect they also represented a large portion of the new job backlog that we had developed in engineering and planning. The former employee of this firm wanted to do something on his own. He was sure with his skills and our growth plans that there must be something we could do together that would make money for both of us.

Little did he know that he was about to become the first new tactic in our strategic marketing and sales plan. While we had never done anything like this before we decided to hire him with the primary job of working as our customer liaison with his former employer. He still had a good relationship with them, and knew that with a focused effort he could work between the two firms to catch up and get us on time.

This was the beginning of our investment in collaboration that we will cover later in the book. The experiment was successful. We not only caught up but began to get a better flow of the right work so that we could maintain our delivery schedule.

Yes, he was the right person, and yes it was a timing issue, but the lesson to be learned is to not get caught up in the way that things are currently working. You definitely cannot find great solutions 'inside the box'. He now not only manages that original customer but has taken over the management of other customers.

We had developed a new model and it was this first tactic that led to a discovery that unlocked the key to sustainable on time delivery. Our new marketing and sales direction was underway.

What we had not counted on was that it also gave us a way to meet or exceed our customer's requirements in terms of price. In fact price was the key ingredient to it all. Once we discovered the need for a more cooperative or collaborative process with our customers we were on the road to the Holy Grail!

We had changed our point of view and began working with our customers on a more strategic basis. What changed was our way of seeing the process and our understanding how we could permanently improve our ability to meet or exceed customer expectations.

Our old struggle to work with parts packages that only partially fit our capabilities and capacities was a matter of the past. We now focused on working in collaboration with our customers to pre select the right parts on the front end of the processes.

So we changed our mind and began the strategic process of marketing our specific capabilities, selling capacity, and creating solutions by building cells to match customer needs. Now, for the first time, we were working on a strategic basis with our customers.

This new strategic marketing direction changed our approach to the sales process.

In the past sales primarily consisted of keeping up customer relations, receiving RFQ and PO's from the customer and trying to come up with competitive pricing. In the new model sales to current customers consists primarily in quoting larger packages and working with engineering and planning to create cellular solutions. It also consists of identifying new prospective customers who are good partners and have enough of 'our type of work' that we can succeed together. As a result this strategic process has opened the way for the rest of our other RTM elements to succeed.

What would we suggest that you do to begin to take advantage of our discoveries and growth in the marketing and sales areas? The following will provide you with some ideas.

- Core Customer Model – What attributes would you like to see in a core customer?

- Core Part(s)/ Assemblies Model – What are the types of parts and assemblies that fit your resource capabilities?

- Core Customer Partner Value Model – What do they require in terms of a supplier and how can you deliver it?

While most traditional organizations market their machinery and fixed plant you should market your ability to make the selected customer more competitive. This is what they want. In addition to risk aversion they want organizations that will focus on their needs to constantly become more competitive. This should be your 'brand' and all you do in you marketing and sales activities should speak to it.

Chapter Four will introduce you to the operational excellence part of our transformational story.

CHAPTER SUMMARY AND KEY TAKE-AWAY POINTS

- Begin your journey on the front end of the process with branding, marketing and sales.

- Work with the customer at the strategic as well as the traditional tactical level.

- Develop a model for the customer and types of work that you want to attract.

- Market and sell your ability to make your customers more competitive.

- Offer cost savings in advance of requests.

CHAPTER FOUR
OPERATIONAL EXCELLENCE

4

With the customer setting the price the wrong organizational point of view will lead to the wrong outcome. As stated in the previous chapter we believe that most companies embark on the development of operational excellence with the wrong point of view. They think that through operational excellence alone they will meet their customer needs. Further they think it will be sustainable. We think a singular focus on operational excellence is the wrong point of view of the Transformational Journey. We too had initially started in this direction. What we discovered in the Roberts Journey was that at some point along the way we went in a different direction. This change in direction was due to our changed point of view. It is this change of path that we think made our journey successful. A change in our point of view was the catalyst. It allowed us to create a transformation that included, but was not exclusively dependent on, operational excellence. What this change in point of view and thinking can do for you is the difference between success and failure. Let's take a look at a tale of a typical journey and the motivations behind it.

A Tale of Two Pathways

Once upon a time a company was challenged by changes in the environment. Customers had changed, demand changed, and the rules they had been used to changed.

The leader of the company began to search for a solution and, in the case of aerospace manufacturing it came in the form of a new way of operating. This new way was called Lean.

The company had been told by its customers that if they didn't get with it and adopt lean they would not be a supplier in the future. But the leader also thought that if they could ever be consistently on time and achieve high levels of quality they could charge whatever they wanted for their parts.

So the company moved toward lean out of both necessity and greed. It moved not to become more competitive, but rather to survive and perhaps take financial advantage of new levels of performance.

Still, the leader was reluctant. He knew that change was difficult. It would take a great amount of energy and time. He had to find a solution that would not require a lot of his time. He was already busy and did not have the time or desire to learn a new way. The company knew it had to change but none of the managers in the organization had the foggiest idea on how to begin.

Like the leader, they were busy and were not motivated to learn lean or to try to transform the company. So, the leader and his team searched the world far and wide for one who knew of this new arcane science. They located and hired a lean guru who had helped many begin their journey.

The lean guru, with the company in tow, embarked on the journey. What the guru advised at the onset was to leave their old ways behind.

They, as the leaders of the company, would first have to commit and change their ways. The guru knew that without letting go of the past one cannot have a successful journey to the future. But they did not hear him. So the leader and his management team left on the journey bringing along with them their old and preferred way of operating.

The old way was there, just in case they needed it. They hid it away in the recesses of their minds and kept quiet about it lest the guru get wise to their trick.

As the journey began the first step was to learn a little about lean and start off with a plan to get better organized. The lean technique they learned was to 6S (sort, set in order, shine, set standards, sustain the change, and safety) their operation. This would at least get them organized.

Next they began to analyze the time element involved with their production floor processes. This led to some changes in the processes and locations of tools and other supporting items.

So far so good, but they still were operating with old ideas and had kept many of them in reserve in case they needed to beat a hasty retreat.

The leader was the worst. He knew intellectually that the new way was best but did not want to change. He liked the way he operated and he liked his point of view. It was comfortable.

His strategy was to try to fit lean ideas into his old way of operating. He would use lean where it suited him but was not yet fully committed to changing his personal point of view.

Next the guru had them create a Kaizen Newspaper that contained all of the action plans for improvement. All of this he did as a part of the process for moving them toward the idea of building cells. This was his plan and they were headed in that direction.

Until this time the company had continued to operate partially in lean mode and partially in the old way. Full commitment was yet to be realized. The leader and his team had only partially committed to the process and were reluctant to spend more company time on it. The culture remained unchanged.

The company now arrived at a mid point in their journey. This occurred when they built their first cell. The guru was more wise and powerful than they even knew. He had introduced them to an entirely new way of thinking.

The problem, however, was that they had not left their old ways behind. The promise of a cell was great but when mixed with an unchanged culture and a mixed production of thought process it did not work. The owners thought they could use the new cell idea to improve their customer performance and then charge whatever they could get away with. The employees were still not committed. They could not see how the new cell would allow them to meet their daily production goals. The cell thought process was too different for them.

It was not too long after that when their journey slowed and then came to a halt. What had gone wrong?

They had an opportunity to become more productive and had built a couple of cells. The problem was that they could not always get to the price their customers wanted with a cell solution. But why?

The problem was three fold.

First the leadership had not fully committed to the change. They had not left their old ways behind.

Second the employees did not fully understand the new way. They had not been properly prepared. Failure and retreat to the old way was a consideration.

And last, but not least, they had not gained the cooperation of their customers to provide them with a flow of the right kind of work for their cells.

Listening to failure stories of lean journeys seems to be more prevalent than stories of success. Roberts was fortunate to have embarked on the journey with a different thought process that allowed them to successfully transform operationally with lean principles. This is where the Roberts pathway departs from most.

The Roberts Journey

Where others struggled and stalled on their journey Roberts solved the problems and moved forward. In the preceding story the company had three problems that stopped them dead in their tracks. So how did Roberts avoid these and other impediments to lean transformation?

The Role of Lean Thinking at Roberts

At Roberts we knew at the onset of the process that we were going to need an open mind. We knew that in order to overcome any of the obstacles to our transformation we would first have to think differently. This new way of thinking that we adopted was lean thinking. Lean thinking is focused on decreasing waste in order to increase speed. For us this was easy as this was the way that the leader had naturally thought for a long time (It was these principles which had allowed him to see the journey in a different light). What do these principles tell us that would allow us to overcome obstacles along the way? While the generally understood lean goals of waste reduction and increased throughput are foremost the following are some of the basic ideas behind our version of lean thinking

(Note: While we don't use these in a formal manner they do represent the key elements of any lean solution process.)

- Learn

- Prepare

- Collaborate

- Reframe

- Experiment

- Conclude

- Continuous Improvement

This is a visual process. First you learn to see the problems or opportunities visually. This allows one to see all of the interconnections and interdependent relationships. This allowed Roberts to see how the employees would respond in advance of the changes. This confirmed in our minds that if we did not commit and lead the way that the employees would not follow. We also were able to see what would happen if we did not leave our old way behind, or get them to do the same. So having the ability to see the global context of the situation visually is essential to a successful journey.

Next we prepared. As we discussed in the beginning of the book, preparation is the step that most organizations overlook. Most organizations, and their leaders, have the tendency to launch prematurely. They are so eager to get it done that they inadvertently create the basis for their own failure. Action without commitment and preparation is a poor strategy. This part of our process helped us to prepare the employees for the amount of change they would have to embrace for a successful transformation. They learned about change in general and how to cope with it successfully. It required new thinking on their part and they had to buy into it if we were to be successful.

We learned about the change process. This helped us to understand the different phases of acceptance that the employees would experience. It made us wiser and armed us with the tools that we needed to make the change process work.

Next collaboration was addressed. One does not transform in a vacuum. We knew that we could not successfully complete our journey alone. Support and assistance would be needed along the way. Collaboration came in several ways. First it came to us in the form of our membership in an Industry Association that was promoting transformation. We decided that we needed to participate in this group at the highest level possible. We had to be willing to put the most in to receive the most from collaboration. After visualizing our participation, connections, flow of ideas and assistance we accepted a position on the board of this organization. This allowed us to exchange ideas and create new directions that would have a major impact on our successful journey. Not only were we able to collaborate at a high level with our customers but we also collaborated with our supply chain. Using visual tools we were able to develop new and more effective lean processes that would impact on our ability to deliver our Custormer Value Proposition.

Reframing is the power element in the lean thinking equation. It provides new insights based on how we see the problems or opportunities. We use several techniques to achieve this part of the process. One is the quality tool of the "Five Whys" (ask 'why' five times). When faced with a new situation we ask these until we have reframed the original problem or opportunity statement so we can see a new path to innovative solution development. We often use simple brainstorming techniques. Again, we will create a problem/opportunity statement. We will then, in a group, begin to generate ideas by association. When we arrive at one idea (or a group) that we think has promise we stop and using that idea (or ideas) reframe the original statement. We then begin again. We keep repeating this process until we arrive at a new and more effective way of seeing what is going on. We know that we have to change the way we see things before embarking on any action.

Experimentation is our way of testing a new idea so that we can reasonably predict its success in advance of a full commitment. Rapid prototyping is another way of stating this part of the lean thinking process. Lean principles are always in the foreground of these experiments and our objective is to achieve the best result. The key is to move forward quickly and do more hands on R&D work. This is a much overlooked area for transformation in many supplier organizations.

Once we have developed our new solution from our lean thinking process we lock down the idea. A champion, or process owner, is assigned that insures that we keep moving forward in seeking improvements.

These represent our general processes for lean progress. As stated in the introduction to this book we had four operational goals. Two of these related to lean. The elimination of set up time and the utilization of equipment were keys to our achieving our transformational objectives. These were realized in the cell model. By creating a flow of the right work over a long period of time we could both eliminate set up time and insure the maximum utilization of our equipment. These support our continuous improvement efforts.

The Pathway Taken

Taking up our story once again, and armed with our new way of lean/cell thinking, we took a somewhat different path. We had prepared well and indoctrinated the employees into lean concepts. In our business model review we had identified the key issue that was constraining the power of most cell solutions. The answer was to first locate the work then build the cell. Most organizations have the process backwards. If you start with operational excellence you are prone to build cells around what appear to be families of parts that you currently produce. While this may work it is not a guarantee that the cell will succeed. The best way to succeed is to first obtain the right work and then build cells as solutions. As the first step take what you currently are good at producing profitably, and approach your current or new customers for more of that type of work. You hit pay dirt when you find a customer that has a lot of that type of work and the need to find a better solution. You don't build the cell until after you model the solution to meet the customer competitive requirements, and gain the customer's commitment. Demand must precede cell construction.

The bigger the demand, the bigger the opportunity. This allows you to adopt a new lean pricing strategy. Based on the waste reduction and equipment utilization you can provide the customer with the pricing they require while at the same time providing you with your profit objectives. This new thinking is driven by the cell concept that gave us an entirely new way to be more competitive. Remember that you need to get enough of the right kind of business to front load your company so you can bring the real power of the cell strategy into play. The traditional process of 'build it and they will come' is too big a risk for any Lean Transformation Process.

The 'one part at a time' bid process is not lean and cannot connect with a lean solution. As partners, the organization and their customers, have to work together to identify new larger packages of families or parts. The first time that Roberts tried this new process it did not work. We had left the customer with what we thought was a full understanding and agreement in terms of the new way of doing business. We were surprised when a week later, from our customer's procurement department we received the same type of transmittal we had always gotten but now it was just bigger. The customer still had submitted a package of 'disconnected parts' but now thousands of them. After a return trip, and several meetings later, we were able to lean out the process and now have it well underway with this customer. Since then we have succeeded more times than we have failed. The new lean cell and pricing model has taken hold.

Another change in our thinking occurred about the same time. While others had successfully adopted cells they had done so out of fear or just to make themselves more profitable. Unlike the competition we had adopted a different point of view. We had come to fully embrace the cell idea and had left our old ways behind. We now knew that there were ways to exploit the cell strategy that we had not even begun to explore. This was the crucial point that made our potential success possible. Our focus changed from us to the customer and our cell concept was the lean solution engine. It was a new belief, that with a focus on continually improving our lean pricing model, we could profitably deliver on our customer value proposition. Our new competitive strategy of lean pricing coupled with advanced cell design/build moved us away from the sole dependence on operational excellence to a new strategy that would give us and our customers a sustainable unfair advantage. We had come to fully embrace this new way of thinking. Since then this great strategic pairing of cell and customer point of view has driven our success.

So the moral of our tale is that the journey can be successful if you change your point of view. We aligned our point of view with the customer. That made us partners and not adversaries. As long as our point of view remains in the service of the customer we cannot fail.

Chapter Five will provide an insight into the human asset part of a successful transformational journey. It contains ideas gained from our experience and new concepts that we have developed along the way.

CHAPTER SUMMARY AND KEY TAKE-AWAY POINTS

- Lean thinking is necessary if you are going to continually improve your performance.

- We used cells as our primary lean tactic to create a situation with sustainable on time delivery and quality.

- First you find the need (families of parts and/or assemblies) and then you create and build the cell.

- Most organizations incorrectly focus on the internal operations first and build cells in advance of securing a flow of parts.

- Front end load the company with the right work that fits your unique capabilities by finding and developing the right customers.

- The key elements of lean thinking at Roberts are as follows

  o Learn

  o Prepare

  o Collaborate

o Reframe

o Experiment

o Conclude

o Continually Improve

Brad's Last Word

"Creativity, or applied imagination, is the source of all new improvement ideas."

CHAPTER FIVE
HUMAN ASSETS AND ORGANIZATION

5

*How do I
establish and
maintain a
process for
selecting,
developing and
organizing the
best human
assets?*

Since the customers set the price it is imperative
that you have the best human assets working for
your organization. This was our company's 'blind
spot'. When we hired the consultant to help us with
the strategy portion of our transformation he asked
us where we wanted to begin. As owners we all
agreed that working with employees was the one
area where we had a weakness. We had little in the
way of a formal job description or performance

evaluation system. No formal training and development process or program existed. Further we had no way to find, locate, hire and develop our most important asset which was our people. There was no management team development process. As we started to get into this area we decided that we would introduce the consultant to the management team and ask him to sit in on one of our weekly staff meetings. After the meeting we asked for his comments. His reply told us that we had a long way to go. While to us it seemed that we, the owners, had a great meeting he had another opinion. Apparently we asked and answered all of the questions in the meeting. We were not using our assets correctly! He discussed with us the role of the management team. The team was supposed to be able to run the company on an operational basis without the involvement of the owners. Wow, with our dictatorial attitude of being the expert in all areas this would require a tremendous change in both our attitude and actions. At that time most all of the owner's activities were operational. We were told that we were doing work that someone else should be doing and it was our job to identify that work and coach others to take it over. Only then would we have time to do our work. Our work is the strategic work of the organization which is work that no one else can do. We needed to move away from making the organization dependent on us. This was necessary in order to make room on our schedule for the more important strategic and transformational work and activities. If we did give up all of what we had been doing operationally what would we do? The consultant told us we would be doing more important work. What was that work and how good would we be at doing it? Starting with the president of the company the consultant began to work with us to make this transition. That was a few years ago. At this time we can report that the transition was successful and we are doing less operational work. While some of us have retained some operational routine it is out of choice and not necessity. Our focus as owners is now primarily strategic.

In regards to the employees we decided to take baby steps. To begin, we picked an area that we had wanted to attack for some time. This was the area of performance based compensation. We had wanted to develop some form of employee compensation where we could reward exceptional performance based on increases in productivity. We wanted to grow the company without an incremental growth in employee numbers. The consultant proposed a gain sharing program. This program was designed to measure the improvement of the Sales Per Employee (SPE) over a period of time. As the percentage improved the employees would share in the gain as a portion of that improvement related to sales. The process included meetings where the employees would share their ideas for improvement along with an individual suggestion system. While it seemed straightforward we were challenged to communicate how it worked to the employees. In the end we were successful in communicating the essence of the program and proceeded with implementation. We ran the program for several years and it worked well for both the employees and Roberts. Productivity increased in most periods as represented by the SPE. While some of this was due to our investment in technology and cells we looked on the process as a partnership with the employees.

While some of the increase in SPE was not due to their individual, or team efforts, a lot of it was and we needed to accept that fact. It never hurt us to allow them to share in the whole gain. In fact it helped us as they knew that the process was more than fair. Since then we have changed and improved the performance based compensation program. As time went on we needed to focus on more specific areas of performance gain and have modified our approach to achieve that end. We achieved an important objective and now are moving toward a greater focus by the owners on the strategic issues facing the company. While important, however, these two initiatives alone would not take us to where we needed to be in terms of managing our portfolio of human assets in a more effective manner. We found that we did not have the knowledge or skills in this area. We struggled to improve. It was not until we hired a new president that this aspect of our operation began to blossom. The new president had a strong skill set in the employee and organizational development areas. Since his hire we have gone from a mediocre firm in these areas to one that has the potential to be 'best in class'. We answered our need in the human asset area by seeking and hiring a top human asset.

What follows are some of the myths in the human asset area that we discovered on our transformational journey. We hope that by sharing these with you we can make a positive impact on how you see this aspect of the transformation process.

The Dual Myth of Wages:

Hire low and pay as little as possible for any employee. Hire at the lowest possible level of competency and let the market dictate what you will pay and not a dollar more. (Otherwise you are leaving money on the table.). Some have called this the 'cheap approach'.

This is a good way to get only the mediocre employees who will create work for you. Hire high and pay more and you increase your odds of winning! It is an investment and not an expense.

The Recruiting Myth

If I advertise in the media I will get the type of employees that I want and need for my firm.

This may work occasionally but the types of employees that you want to hire are gainfully employed by others and are probably not looking for a job. You need to find a way to get to them. We have employees recommend others and profile people who they think would make good employees that they meet at industry gatherings and outside training sessions.

The Performance Evaluation Myth

Evaluations are a necessary evil and the employees always associate them with a raise in wages.

At Roberts we have come to understand that, done properly, employee evaluations can drive performance change. In fact that is the primary goal of a performance evaluation process. Employees will always associate them with raises if you let them. It is the responsibility of leadership and management to make the system robust. We found that an annual evaluation is not enough to make the system work. On going short form evaluations can give interim feedback that keeps the system dynamic.

The Employee Rank Myth

Employees are not as important as the other stakeholders, customers and suppliers.

A scheduled meeting with an employee is as important as for any other stakeholder. We don't cancel meetings or otherwise give our employees any reason to feel that they are not important to us. It is the employee who will make our performance possible and we must recognize them and the value that they can bring to the work place. We respect them.

The Indirect vs. Direct Employee Myth

We want as few indirect employees as possible and when we hire them we don't want to pay them very much.

The world has changed and now some of the indirect employees are required to build and maintain relationships with customers. Properly organized they are the glue that holds operations and relationships together.

The Working Manager Myth

We want managers that roll up their sleeves and work on the machines.

If the managers are working on the machines you are not getting much return on your investment. While from time to time it may be necessary for a manager to roll up their sleeves you don't want them constantly doing so. If they are 'doing' rather than 'managing' they are failing. This change to a management perspective is one of the transitions that signal a movement to the next level of performance for any organization. When you move from the old model of the 'working manager' to the one of the 'leader manager' you are on your way!

The Jobs Myth

In our industry we hire people based on their ability to do a job.

This has changed as employees today expect to have some potential for growth and movement. If you hire strictly to do jobs and not for potential growth and movement you are missing an opportunity. Along with this goes the idea of careers. A company that has careers, and career paths, has much more to offer the 'best' prospective employees. Given a choice the best employees will always migrate to a place where they have a structure for promotion and growth.

The Training and Development Myth

As required we make training available but still place most of the responsibility for success on the employee.

The modern organization and its culture require that employees constantly grow through training and development activities. It is a joint responsibility of the employee and the organization. The informed organization will not allow this important part of the organizational development process to be the sole responsibility of the employee. The objective is to work with the employee to build their value.

Dispelling these myths has helped us to shape our human asset approach. It is a form of talent management. Our system now addresses all of these areas in a structured and consistent manner. We want to be the employer of choice. That is how we wish to brand our company from an employee perspective.

Chapter Six will present the elements that we found that our Leader needed to work on for transformational success.

CHAPTER SUMMARY AND KEY TAKE-AWAY POINTS

- We manage human assets and not human resources – it is a qualitative change in thinking.

- The owners have to find a way to make the business independent of them operationally so they can concentrate on strategic work.

- Pick a starting point to work on the development of your human assets where you think you and the employees can gain the most in the short term. We picked performance based compensation and increased productivity.

- Review the employee myths that you are operating under and test them to see if they are in your best interest.

- Recruiting, hiring, organizing and developing employees require a specialized skill set that you have to develop or otherwise secure to make any transformation possible. We hired the expertise.

Brad's Last Word

"Most employees are only fifty percent productive and it is the job of the leader to find and release the other fifty percent."

TRANSFORMATIONAL LEADERSHIP

6

*What knowledge
and personal
skills does the
leader need to
have and to
understand in
order to
successfully lead
a transformation?*

In an industry where the customers are setting
the price an effective organization needs great
transformational leadership. We found that the first
step toward our lean transformation had to be taken
by me. I would suggest that you do not attempt to
transform your company unless you have read and
understood the leadership attributes that follow.
The first leadership step toward success for any
transformation initiative is to change the culture of

your firm and build new cultural equity. The culture must understand and embrace the transformational ideas and concepts. The leader must first prepare him or herself. The leader must change first!

We found that there were six leadership and cultural elements involved in creating, implementing and sustaining our lean transformation. These are as follows.

1. Commitment – to oneself, the firm and the stakeholders

2. Passion – for the cause.

3. Time Management – The leader's personal agenda.

4. Leadership Team Development – Teaching others to manage and develop.

5. Organizational Development – What is the best way to organize the human assets?

6. Business Model Development – Creating a viable and flexible/ adaptable business

model around which brand leadership can be developed.

COMMITTMENT

Any successful cultural transformation begins with commitment. Commitment means that you will do whatever is necessary to meet your responsibilities. In this case it is a responsibility to increase your customer's competitiveness and your profit by transforming your business assets and systems. Once committed you must persevere and not back off or let yourself 'off the hook'. We suggest that you not try this alone. It is always better to lead in teams than as an individual. If everyone on the team is committed then it is less likely that any one member, including the boss, will back down. For if you do back down it will betray employee confidence. Through commitment and action the employees need to see that you are sincere. Not following through on commitment to change will make it impossible to motivate the employees to embrace the new way of thinking. Change begins at home and you must be ready to follow through on your commitment.

PASSION

Passion brings in the elements of purpose and meaning. Why am I doing this and what will it mean to me and my company? The leader and the leadership team must think this through; for without passion the leader will not be able to sustain the energy required to see the journey through to the end. So the answers to the two questions of 'why' and 'what' are a pre requisite to a successful plan and execution. At Roberts we are not doing this just for us but for the industry, the country and the global economy. We see ourselves as pioneers of new and better ways to create value. We want to break down old paradigms and their associated costs in order to positively and permanently impact the aerospace industry performance. This is the legacy that we want to create and it drives us in all we do.

TIME MANAGEMENT

A Lean approach to time management is different than most. As you know lean is about waste and speed. As a lean practitioner you want to eradicate waste and therefore increase the speed of the throughput of your company. In order to do this effectively you have to start with your own work habits and activities. You should approach time management as a process. As a process the first step might be to create a Personal Value Stream Map (A work flow map of all of the key categories of work you do) and a list of your daily Standard Work activities. Next you examine the map and list of standard work items to find out which items are creating or causing bottlenecks in your work process. These are the ones that do not 'flow' but rather are constricting both the amount and the quality of your daily work output. Once you have identified your personal bottlenecks and key constraints you begin to eradicate waste and therefore increase your personal productivity and contribution to the company. You take them on one at a time. Start with the one that will have the greatest immediate impact on your contribution. This is where you will want to free up the constraint and begin to achieve more quality time in the process.

Brad's Tip on Time Management

Time management, in its best form, has been one area where I have endeavored to build a core strength. I realized that I needed to continually improve in this area in order to be able to maintain or improve my personal level of performance. I have always been able to sort out the most important from the least important tasks. I am also a big picture person. This means that I have often left the details to others.

As I moved forward in my pursuit of improvement I developed new strategies and tactics to support this endeavor and strengthen my attention to detail and follow up. My first such tactic was to hire a personal assistant.

I looked for a person who had the skill set that matched my time management blind spots. My initial plan was to give this person all of the detail work on the computer. That worked to a point and I began to generate more work product in less time. What I found out in the end was that I needed to give up my planning, scheduling and follow up completely in order to gain the most from my assistant.

In addition I let the assistant manage my (our) calendar. This person makes sure that I deliver on my commitments and that I am prepared for every meeting and presentation. It is truly a 1+1=5. A personal assistant, properly trained and empowered, is the best way for an executive to gain time. It is an investment and not an expense in improving the quantity and quality of executive time.

LEADERSHIP TEAM DEVELOPMENT

Work on leadership team development naturally follows work on time management by the leader. Once the leader's personal work improvement process is underway it is time to begin to build the same knowledge and change initiatives at the leadership team level. The leadership team, with its personal experience of the process, will then be prepared to lead their employees in a successful transformation. The process for the team is the same as that for the leader/ owner. A personal value stream map, as described in the previous section, is created by each team member. Then a team Value Stream Map is created for the team's work product. This map constitutes the inputs, value add activities and outputs for the work of the team. From this the processes are improved and the team member's standard work and time management development programs are undertaken. In addition the leader and the team work together on team building. The core element in this work is cooperation. The usual element at the core of team member relationships is competition. Recognizing this situation, the leader refocuses them on cooperation. The team members learn how to focus on a theme of service to one another and implement a team building process that fosters that theme. Once this work, from a cooperative service perspective, is underway the leader and the team are ready to tackle their shared work at the organizational level.

Brad's Leadership Team Member Development Story

I have developed a new understanding of leadership team member compensation. It is based on the premise that what the team member can contribute is primary. What they cost is secondary. The key is their ability to make a contribution that exceeds their cost.

If you hire based on market costs (How little can I pay?) you may hire someone who costs you more than they can contribute. You still need to have a thorough selection process but you should never restrict the prospects based on a minimal compensation package.

I learned this valuable lesson about a third of the way into my 10 year journey and it has greatly influenced my ability to attract and build a top notch leadership team. My first hire from this point of view came from one of my customers.

I knew intuitively that the person was a great hire but the price tag initially bothered me. I went with my gut instinct and have never regretted the hire. Once I had this one underway I hired a new quality manager. Again I paid more than I had wanted to pay. Again it paid off. I have never looked back.

I now understand that many a company is held back because of their reluctance to step up their compensation packages to match their needs. My last great hire was my replacement as the president of the company. He embodies the character and leadership that any company would seek in this key position.

He is the first non family member to reach this level in our company. We had to change our mind not only in regards to compensation but also in regards to a family dependent firm. That is another step up for us that will help to guarantee the perpetuity of our organization.

We are no longer bound to the hope that some family member might be both motivated and qualified for the job. We have moved beyond that and with it came the healthy development of our leadership team.

ORGANIZATIONAL DEVELOPMENT

Approaching organizational development from a lean perspective provides a unique opportunity to increase performance. Again using the lean tools the leader will gain new insight and a more effective approach to managing the development of the organization for the transformed enterprise. This approach allows reframing the traditional organizational concepts. A key question is 'How can we best organize to have the least amount of waste thus increasing our productivity'? A value stream map of organizational activities will suggest new arrangements of departments, jobs and other organizational entities. This work will eradicate waste and improve connections and communications within and without the organization. It will also suggest new ways to connect the organization more effectively. New ways to organize may be developed that could provide a competitive advantage. All of this activity is aimed at an organizational development program that will increase sales per employee, and create more purposeful work and jobs. Add to this an effective career-centered employee training, development and recognition system and you will have a new and more effective organization. It will also incorporate the goals of a transformational approach which include more meaning and purpose to all that you do.

Brad's Organizational Development Story

In order to maximize performance a good business model needs a complimentary organizational model. My first real insight into the power of organizational strategy came as a result of three situations. These were slow release of jobs to the shop floor, increasing customer requests for engineering consultation and a PEER Group Strategy Session on Value Stream Mapping.

What I discovered was that we, as others in our sector of business, had a weak front end organization. We did not have enough horsepower in the engineering and planning phase of the business to take advantage of the cell strategy and lean operation that we had created. So we went to work on this area and used the lean cell development model ideas to build up our engineering and planning areas.

We now have included the engineering and planning operations and their work in our planning packages. All activities in this area are designated operations and the employees in this area log in and out of all engineering and planning work.

In addition we have hired new engineering and planning staff to support the basic staff that had served us so well in the past. While holding engineers accountable for time management is not an easy task, it has helped us once again to develop a new competitive edge.

BUSINESS MODEL DEVELOPMENT

The last thing that the Leader tackles is the business model development process. Once the management team and organizational work is underway, and the culture is changing, it is time to reflect on the business model. The business model is the way that the company makes money. It also serves as the foundation for the company's branding program. A good business model consists of several elements that are interrelated to make up a composite model for the firm. Taking a lean cell perspective to the business model development and deployment creates a model with the following elements.

The Lean Customer Value Proposition

- **Perfect Products** – What customers need?

- **Perfect Services** – Transparent information provided on time.

- **Perfect Price** – to make customers competitive.

- **Perfect Innovation**
    – Tracking improvement of all three of the key elements – to continually enhance our Customer Value Proposition AND A DECISION ON WHAT TO BE THE BEST AT

IN THE WORLD. This last piece is the key. If you are not best at anything then you will be dealing only in a commodity environment and will restrict your level of performance and sustainable earnings. It is important to be operationally excellent but it is quite another thing to be dependent on that one skill for your profits.

- **Perfect Profit** – a profit equation based on selecting the profit percentage first and then working back into the expense model that will generate it.

Brad's Business Model Development Story

Business Models are my hobby. I am always fascinated by new ways to create customer value that also meet or exceed the sustainable profit needs of an organization. This was the point of view that I used when I recognized that a cell was in fact a small business. If I modeled cells financially and provided each with a good business model then I gained an advantage over my competition.

While most organizations see cells from the point of view of making parts, I saw them from the point of view of making money. It was using them as revenue/ profit generators that gave me a distinct advantage. To me it was a given that if you could create standard work you could improve quality and on-time delivery.

I accepted this and moved on to create cells and work with them as my primary financial strategy. This was the strategy that would allow me and my customers to become more competitive. My next step was to look beyond my immediate environment to find other applications for my new cell strategy. I am constantly looking at the Aerospace supply chain for more ways to leverage the cellular idea. I do this while continually improving the cells that we have in place throughout our company. Cells are how I win and they are the backbone of the supply chain strategies that I am developing.

___

These are the lessons of the leader. What follows is a list of goals for the leader to adopt in each of these areas. It is a sample 'to do' list to help anyone who wishes to move forward as the leader in their company's transformation.

THE LEADER'S GOALS

Goal One - The Transformation Commitment List – It is documented and presented to all of the stakeholders.

1. Leaders Commitment – To lead by example in the execution of the leaders standard work activities. These are the specific work activities that are focused on the transformation of the company.

2. The Commitment to the Company – The commitment is to build value through on going improvement of sales and productivity.

3. The Commitment to the Stakeholders – The commitments to the employees, customers, suppliers and the public is to build value through on-going improvement in all resources.

Goal Two - The Lean Time Management List – established and maintained for the leaders and all management personnel.

1. Personal value stream map/ standard work development.

2. Identification of personal bottlenecks and key constraints

3. Action plans to permanently overcome key constraints.

Goal Three - The Lean Organization Building List

1. Organizational Review– To move from a 'flat' organizational structure where all employees

may report to the leader to one that operates through a management team. The organizational structure should create results for the customer and report through the management team to the leader.

2. Management and Employee Team Building – Create and conduct training and events that facilitate the building of a self motivated and directed workforce.

3. Team Accountability – In a lean managed organization the teams take responsibility for actions and results (no excuses).

4. Personal Accountability – In a lean managed organization individuals take responsibility for actions and results (no excuses).

Goal Four - The Management Team Building List

1. Teaching the Culture – A non judgmental culture based on positive approaches and respect.

2. Changing Minds and Hearts – Aligning the individual with the culture through education and rewards.

3. Teaching the idea of Flow – Teaching the necessity for all processes to flow in one direction, and to slow down all of the processes to the proper pace in order to speed up the throughput (output in sales) for the customer.

4. Running the Business on a Plan – The discipline of following a map instead of 'wandering' toward goals and objectives.

Goal Five - The Lean Business Model List

1. The Business Model Elements – To develop an effective and responsive customer value proposition, and profit, resources, processes and innovation models.

2. Creating with Pixie Dust – Here pixie dust refers to that magic imaginative lean thinking that allows a leader to create continual enhancement, innovation and strategies to provide the

customer with ever increasing value and profit for the organization.

3. Business Model Performance – To develop a scorecard to measure the key performance factors for the organization.

The following chapter is a discussion on how you can become the competition.

CHAPTER SUMMARY AND KEY TAKE-AWAY POINTS

- The Leader must first change and then lead the way in a fully engaged manner.

- The five leadership and cultural elements – Key areas for attention.

  o Commitment

  o Time Management

  o Management Team Development

  o Organizational Development

  o Business Model Development

- The Leader's Goal List – What a leader needs to develop to begin to transform the company.

  o Goal One - The Lean Commitment

  o Goal Two – The Lean Management List

  o Goal Three – The Lean Organization Building List

  o Goal Four – The Lean Management Team Building List

o Goal Five – The Lean Business Model List

Brad's Last Word

"A successful and sustainable transformation must be led."

CHAPTER SEVEN
BECOMING THE COMPETITIVE LEADER

7

How do I
address the area
of competition
in my
transformation
process?

Since the customer is setting the price you always want to make sure that you are the benchmark organization. This is how you stay in control of your destiny. Being pursued by the competition as the industry benchmark has always been our goal. That is what our journey and this chapter are all about. We always knew that whatever commitment we made would be worth the time, effort and resources if we could become the benchmark organization that everyone wanted to emulate. We would set the mark and keep advancing it. That was and has been our mantra.

How did we do this? We did it with the mindset that anything is possible and everything can always be done better. In short we embrace CHANGE... We improve everything we do and in the end it results in Roberts becoming the competition or brand leader.

What does a brand leader look like? From a results perspective a brand leader is one that gets chosen at the MOMENT OF SELECTION. From a business development perspective there are three areas for development in order to achieve this distinction.

- **Brand Strategies** – create the most meaningful methods to craft more value.

- **Brand Expressions** – create the most effective way to express who we are and the value we represent.

- **Brand Innovations** – create the most unique on a continual basis.

From a Brand Strategy Development perspective the brand leader wants to work on two areas. The first is brand equity. The key question is 'what strategies can I develop that will contribute the most to the equity of my brand?' Here equity refers to its worth. This means that I have to work on the most difficult problems and issues facing customers in our industry. I cannot become a brand leader if I do not work on the most perplexing issues. Any solutions that I generate for difficult problems will allow me to create new and disruptive strategies that will enhance my brand and thus add to its equity. This is also a necessity. If I am to become, and maintain my status, as the brand leader then it is necessary to attack those areas that are in need of a new direction.

The second part of my strategic work is focused on addressing the emotional issues facing my customers. I need to develop new insights into those issues that can allow me to fashion the most effective strategies. These are those insights that lead to assisting others to reach their goals and objectives. While this is focused on customers it is also an area that I need to address in terms of the other members of my supply chain. This means that

I have to develop my emotional intelligence. Emotional intelligence will allow me to interact more effectively with other decision makers and enhance their brand experience.

The Brand Expressions are those tools and actions that I take in order to communicate and embed my brand message. As the brand leader these need to be the best of class. They are a combination of the following.

- **Actual Actions** – How the customer and supply chain experience of my organization.

- **Promotional Activities** – Those things that promote the image of the brand leader.

Actual actions are the way that a customer or supplier experiences my company. Therefore, if I am the brand leader I need to have those experiences be real and be consistent. This will lead to trust and hopefully a selection of my brand before others at the MOMENT OF SELECTION. To reinforce the actual actions I also need to promote my brand with various items and activities. These are all created within the context of my brand promise. The brand promise is the expectation that we want to embed in our customers that can then be met in each transaction. They want and expect to receive a certain product/service offering and experience it in a certain way. We then fulfill this expectation and they begin to trust us. The more they select us and we meet their expectations the more they will select us in the future. The form our brand takes is therefore critical in the setting of our customer and supplier expectations and fulfillment processes.

Brand innovations are those things that we do to enhance our brand. One key area in brand innovation is that of elasticity. This is where we take a successful brand strategy and move it into a new area that lies beyond its original application. This allows us to leverage a successful idea and create more value. What follows is an example of the application of this strategy to one of the key problems that has plagued the aerospace industry for some time.

BRAD'S BRAND STRATEGY STORY

One of the key brand strategies used by Roberts is that of cellular development. This has been at the core of our strategy to make our organization more competitive. I used the cell idea to solve the historical problems created by outside processors of metal parts. Lack of progress in the areas of on time delivery and quality by outside processors were accepted as part of this area of the aerospace supply chain.

A chain is only as strong as its weakest link. This meant that the strength of the chain was heavily dependent on a tier of suppliers that were consistently inconsistent. This was an opportunity for Roberts to be the brand leader. Applying the idea of creating a modular/cellular approach to the key processes allowed us to create an alarmingly new strategy. We used it to develop our own outside processing company. It used new cellular approaches and because of the processes, is capable of consistent and timely results. New value has been added to the overall supply chain. This is what brand leaders accomplish.

Becoming the competition means that you need to have the mind of a brand leader. Instead of running away from difficult problems you meet them head on and solve them. You therefore see problems as opportunities. If others ignore them then they are fair game which allows you to create new brand equity. In addition to being chosen more often than not at the MOMENT OF SELECTION the following are some of the additional advantages of brand leadership.

- You will attract better employees

- You will be able to more effectively address and control industry development.

- You will have the ability to increase profits and business value well above industry norms.

The biggest trap of brand leadership is developing a fixed and defensive mind set. Many a brand leader has fallen based on a 'defend the hill' mentality. This means that along with brand leadership you have to be unrelenting in your desire to continually reinvent yourself. This is at the heart the RTM approach to brand leadership. The next new thing is more important than basking in the spotlight of your brand leadership position.

The other area of concern to a brand leader is to make sure that those that are following are not too far behind. The strength of the industry is dependent on a strong supply chain that can support the needs of all of the customers. Brand leadership therefore requires one to take time to assist others in developing more effective offerings. Giving back time and ideas to the industry is an added responsibility for anyone in a leadership position. Again the idea of contribution and cooperation trumps that of competition.

Brand leadership is the pathway to becoming the competitive leader. The goal is to consistently manage the customer's expectations while addressing their emotional needs to succeed at individual levels. This is the pathway to getting the right orders from the right customers. It allows one to be selective and therefore front end load the company with a flow of pre selected work. It also allows you to sidestep some of the pricing issues in this era of commoditization.

With this chapter the section on the transformation process comes to an end. At Roberts we have embraced the idea that transformation is the most important process and the continued health of our organization is dependent on it. We hope that you will do the same. Next we will move into the section on collaboration. Collaboration has helped us to accelerate our transformational initiatives and has provided new and improved value to our customers. Chapter Eight, the first chapter in this section, will introduce you to the collaboration concept and how we applied it to the need for internal collaboration.

CHAPTER SUMMARY AND KEY TAKE-AWAY POINTS

- Becoming the competitive leader is achieved through a brand leadership process.

- Brand leadership consists of three key elements

  o Brand Strategies based on solutions to big problems and opportunities.

  o Brand Expressions that help to position and embed the brand in the mind of the customer.

  o Brand Innovations that continually add to the brand equity.

- Brand leadership carries responsibilities if you wish to remain in the lead.

  o Helping others in your industry

  o Promoting Cooperation

  o Maximizing your contribution

Brad's Last Word

"Everyone has a brand but most don't know what it is."

PART THREE

COLLABORATION

CHAPTER EIGHT

INTERNAL COLLABORATION

8

How do I use
the idea of
collaboration to
improve internal
operations?

Understanding collaboration and using it is
important in a situation where the customer sets the
price. Before a company can learn to collaborate
externally it must learn to do so internally. Before
that it must learn what collaboration is and how it
applies to any transformational journey. Our RTM
includes a collaboration step. We always work
together internally to innovative ways to make our
customers more competitive. In order to implement
this step we first focused on the culture. As with all
culture changes, we knew that a new belief system

was necessary in order to successfully implement the idea of collaboration. What follows are examples of some traditional beliefs that hinder successful internal collaboration.

- Time: Collaboration slows down action.

- "In Crowd" Point of View: Collaboration does not work because THEY don't understand.

- Fault Finding: I need them to change.

- My Job: Its not my job

- Their Job: When I have finished my part of the job I am done.

- I don't like them: For whatever reason I don't like working with them.

- I don't want to share my knowledge or ideas.

These are just several examples of some potential cultural beliefs that need to be changed in today's organization if any type of successful internal collaboration is to be achieved.

A belief system in favor of collaboration might hold the following beliefs.

- Time: Collaboration is a time saver because we create a better solution the first time.

- "In Crowd" Point of View: We limit our risk if we involve others who think differently than us as we may have blind spots in our thinking.

- Fault Finding: I am a part of the process that is not working so what can I do to change before I ask them to change?

- My Job: My job is to insure that the customer expectations are met and my fellow employees have good ideas that can help me to achieve that objective.

- Their Job: What can I do in my job to make their job easier?

- I don't like them: I don't have to like them but I do need to set my personal feelings aside and have respect for them as human beings and as a part of our organization.

- Sharing of information

Culturally and for the sake of internal collaboration these must represent the new employee mindset.

Next we uncovered another constraint that exists in the area of internal collaboration. The world is moving from a socio economic time where business success was based strictly on logic, detail and knowledge of specialty areas to one where imagination and creative approaches take the forefront. This change in thinking is what businesses will need to succeed in the future. We cannot innovate enough! As this occurs it creates both a need and a new set of issues to solve in terms of internal collaboration. We need more and not less collaborative innovation.

In the past we hired employees who for the most part were educated in the old paradigm of isolated job functions. We now need to change that mind set to one of a shared sense of jobs. We need to foster cooperation and empathy. One way to achieve this is to create employee success plans. These are focused on helping the employees learn new, more global job functions in order to get them out of their narrow job focus. These are not to take the place of performance reviews but are in addition to what is currently being offered to them. It is the first step toward career growth plans. These plans should include examples of what is expected in order to achieve certain levels of performance. Included in these expectations are collaboration skills. In this way collaboration becomes one of the things that they need to learn to do better to succeed. This is all a part of the preparation for the organization wide focus on collaboration.

As with the overall cultural change a focus on internal collaboration must start with the leader and managers of the organization. They must set the example and collaborate on both the transformation changes and the daily operations of the firm. They must operate in a respectful and collaborative environment. If they don't they can never expect the employees to follow. Unilateral decision making, when it affects more than just one department, is not acceptable. Clear communication and other considerate behavior must be displayed. This must all be achieved in preparation for any company wide collaboration effort.

Once the organization has a collaborative leadership environment it can proceed to build it on a company wide basis. From a planning point of view this becomes one of the key elements of the organization's employee development process.

The end result is that you want to move the culture from point A (where it is today) to point B. Point B is where collaboration has become embedded in the culture. All employees collaborate as a regular part of their job. At this point collaboration becomes a valuable asset and can begin to move beyond the borders of the organization.

The next chapter will take us to the next stop on the journey. This is where we discuss our collaborative experiences in relation to our PEER Group.

CHAPTER SUMMARY AND KEY TAKE-AWAY POINTS

- A Cultural paradigm change is required.

   o Old Way – Individual isolated work areas with little contact or concern for others in the organization.

   o The New Way – Internally networked workers that support the flow of information and ideas.

- The need for new innovation requires more collaboration

   o Competitiveness depends on the ability to quickly innovate

   o The group mind holds more potential than unlinked individual minds

   o Culture change is required and the leaders and managers must change first and lead by example.

Brad's Last Word

"Collaboration, and the power of persuasion, are two of the key skills for any employee who wants to succeed in the days ahead."

CHAPTER NINE
PEER GROUP COLLABORATION

9

Where the customer sets the price peer group ideas and support helps to speed the learning and organizational development curve. Peer group collaboration is one way that we have found to leverage our lean transformational expertise and gain useful insights. Being a member of a peer group has been an impetus for us to accelerate our journey and thus our performance. What follows is a discussion of our Peer group objectives, methods and accomplishments.

1. The Mission of our PEER Group - to become world class lean managed organizations by...

   a. Solving industry problems

   b. Sharing best practices

   c. Consulting with each other in regards to specific issues

   d. Specific group initiatives to improve individual member organizational performance

      i. Lean Audits

      ii. Training and Development

      iii. Marketing and Sales

      iv. Financial Management

   e. Making Commitments and Sharing Results/ Holding each other accountable.

   f. Meeting group standards

We are a member of the Southern California Manufacturing Group and have been since its inception. (thescmg.com). This is a group of peer companies that have joined together to assist each other in the pursuit of World Class status. This collaborative effort began years ago. It began as a monthly meeting that rotated between the member companies. At these meetings we would tour, critique and pick up best practice ideas. This initially created a lot of value for all of the members. We then realized there were common issues and problems that we all needed to face that would not be addressed in this format.

At this point we hired a facilitator. He helped us to organize our efforts to jointly solve problems and take advantage of, or create new opportunities. This second stage of development has been fruitful and has seen the development of four sub groups. These groups are focused on specific business activities such as training and development, marketing and sales and financial management and supply chain development. It is at this level that other management employees from each firm work to assist each other in the development of core skills and solutions. In the area of lean there is a lean audit sub group that competes every four months for a trophy and 'bragging rights'. The last two elements of the peer group activities are that of the sharing of results and agreed upon standards of operation. The peer group, through quarterly reviews of performance, allows each member to judge the impact of their work against commitments made to the group. It also allows each of us to compare our performance improvements with other members of the group. Participation in this group has accelerated our lean transformation.

Brad's PEER Group Story

Accountability is a great benefit to be derived from peer group membership. As one of my responsibilities within our group I was given the chairmanship of our marketing and sales sub group. I was asked to help others in the group become more effective in this area. My challenge was to take what I naturally do and develop a process that others could use. Much of my sales and marketing activity had been based on personal involvement with customers. One on one relationship building/ problem solving in a reactionary mode was how I had worked in the past so I was not sure what I needed to do first. I set out to work on this challenge and discovered that the first sales and marketing activity that anyone should do is to put together a data base and analysis of their current customers. Although my company did have some customer lists and data, most of the information resided in the heads of the sales staff. I knew that a more comprehensive data base was important and critical for decision making. Further it would create a lot of value if we were to create a more comprehensive tool. So we did and it was. The ironic thing is that without the peer group accountability for leading this sub group, I would not have naturally reached this conclusion.

Chapter Ten will cover the subject of supply chain collaboration. This is the final element in our collaboration model. It is one that requires the most skill and a new point of view.

CHAPTER SUMMARY AND KEY TAKE-AWAY POINTS

- In a peer group you learn that it is better to give than to receive. You learn more by giving and assisting. The more that you participate the more you get out of it.

- Peer groups can help to accomplish many objectives on a lean journey.

  o Accelerate progress

  o Share and compare best practices

  o Hold each other accountable for progress

  o Collaborate on key problems and opportunities

  o Raise the profile and brand of the company

  o Improve personal skills

  o Create a forum for other managers in the member organizations

Brad's Last Word

"Collaboration and cooperation are more powerful forces than competition in the development of new competitive strategies."

CHAPTER TEN
SUPPLY CHAIN COLLABORATION

10

How can I develop collaboration that helps me improve the supply chain performance?

Supply chain collaboration helps to minimize product cost which is important when the customer is setting the price. We approached this area by first identifying the key collaboration areas. We found that there were three supply chain areas to address in any company's lean journey.

- Managing the Existing Supply Chain

- Enhancing the Current Supply Chain

- Building New Supply Chain Solutions

I made the statement at the beginning of this book that the one who builds the best supply chain wins. This directly contributes to the ability of any supplier to deliver on a customer value proposition. Further it must contribute to the price element in that proposition and it is here that lean strategies come into play.

The traditional strategy that most suppliers use to manage their supply chain is the 'squeaky wheel'. This is far from lean. Always 'following up' is not a process it is a reaction. To deliver on your promise, as a part of the customer value proposition, you will need to get your current supply chain working under a better management strategy. This begins with the creation of supply chain standards of performance. Initially you and your management team develop a set of performance criteria that need to be met in order to deliver on your customer value proposition. Once this is established you measure your current supply chain partners against these standards. This will usually create a performance gap. The next step is to meet with each of the supply chain partners to discuss the standards that you have set and how the two of you can collaborate to improve the performance levels. This joint collaboration, or developmental planning, is a key to understanding this first step in supply chain performance enhancement. If you are in a high demand low supply environment you cannot dictate standards to the suppliers. So whatever improvements you need to accomplish will need to be presented in a win/win fashion. In some cases there are changes that you can make on your end that can enhance the performance or help your supply chain partner. In all cases you should seek to understand the problem fully and approach the improvement plans in a positive manner. Lastly someone needs to own the supply chain process. This person is responsible not only for the current operational performance but also for the continual improvement of the chain.

Some current supply chain partners may not be amenable to performance enhancements or change. In that case you will need to develop new partners. This process is the same as recruiting employees. Your supply chain process owner should have a process underway to continually locate and negotiate with new and better suppliers. This type of active process will insure that you have the best supply chain situation at any given point in time.

Developing a preferred supplier program can also prove beneficial. Since you have established standards of performance you can use them to identify and qualify new partners. A goal for new and better suppliers should be set as an element of your annual Strategic Plan. Along with this goal you need a scorecard that you use to both evaluate and communicate with your suppliers. This type of constant communication is necessary if you are to improve overall supply chain performance.

As a consequence of all of the work that you will put into your supply chain performance enhancement program you will end up with a model for the development of subsequent supply chains. An opportunity from a customer may necessitate the development of a supply chain that is not currently in existence. Your model for doing this, including all of your performance and continual improvement processes is a competitive edge. It will allow you to respond effectively on price, product and service whenever you are faced with a new customer opportunity.

Brad's Supply Chain Story

A peer group member needed some of our skills in the development of a cell solution for one of their customers. Our first step was to meet with them to scope out the extent of the project. We soon realized that this project would go beyond just the creation of a cell. If they were to succeed we would have to assist them in the creation of a dedicated supply chain.

It was not enough to simply create a cell. The production scale and criteria necessitated our involvement in developing a unique supply chain solution. First we lined up the parts of the chain. Once that was accomplished we created the connections and information routes that would be important in the management of the overall chain performance.

The end product was an entire manufacturing plan. This was collaboration at a higher level but was made possible by our cell and supply chain expertise and peer group membership.

Part Four, the conclusion of this book on our Journey, contains three chapters. The first lays out a competitive idea to move Roberts and our customers to the next level.

CHAPTER SUMMARY AND KEY TAKE-AWAY POINTS

- The Three supply chain areas for development

    o Current supply chain

    o Enhancing the existing supply chain

    o Creating new supply chains

- Develop and manage with a process vs. a reaction

    o Establish standards

    o Develop core suppliers

    o Communicate and become the best customer

Brad's Last Word (Repeated!)

"He who has the best supply chain (with no weak links) wins."

PART IV
CONCLUSION

CHAPTER ELEVEN
THE NEXT TRANSFORMATIONAL STEP

11

No. It is only the beginning. At the onset of the book we suggested that the customer sets the prices. Now we will go a step further and suggest that the customer also sets forth the pathway for an organization's strategy development. To be successful one must learn to listen and follow the customer's pathways into the future. This is a transformational idea and is the centerpiece for our change theory of the future. Roberts must change and those changes must continue to be based on our customer's needs and expectations. We need to keep them competitive! As an example if the customer wants to go global then it is our job as a strategic supplier to help them get there successfully. As we speak 'Roberts Global' as an idea is under development. If the customer needs us, as many do today, to become an engineering company then we must pursue that direction. This is where the future lies and it is where Roberts is headed. The following are some key questions. These are a part of our RTM in order to transform ourselves to the next level as a Customer Strategic Partner. Whatever we can do to support our customer's strategies into the future we will do and do it well.

KEY QUESTIONS FOR THE FUTURE

1. What are our customer's key strategies for the future?

2. What are the common customer strategies and which are unique?

3. Which strategies are we currently positioned to support?

4. What do we need to do to expand current strategies?

5. What new assets or competencies do we need to develop to support those strategies?

6. How have we integrated our customer's needs and opportunities into our strategic plan?

7. How much time do we have to prepare to support our customer's direction?

8. How are we communicating our support efforts back to the customer?

9. What new areas of the business or other business do we need to explore to provide further support for our customers?

10. What other questions do we need to be asking ourselves?

Once we have answered these questions we will have an outline of the goals we need to achieve in order to continue to be the most effective low risk supplier organization in our industry. We may also open up in other industry areas in order to meet our customer's needs. Several years ago we built a new organization around the idea of "Cells". This organization has flourished and is a one of a kind thus meeting Warren Buffet's criteria for building franchises. Along with our own cell building this company builds cells to order for other customers. Faced with continuing on time delivery and quality issues in the area of outside part processing we innovated and created a new lean process that resulted in our latest new company mentioned earlier in the book. We built these new companies to be able to meet our customers' needs and requirements for a speedier response. So if you can't find a solution you may need to invent and invest in one. The key is that we cannot stop and have to be diligent at creating a future that will meet the needs of our customers on a sustainable basis. This is not an alternative but a must if we are to continue to succeed.

While we will continue to address these questions as a part of our standard strategic planning cycle, we know that all of our customers need to be successful globally. Rather than letting the global economy evolve on its own we need to protect our interests. We do this by crafting a path that enhances our prosperity while meeting the needs of our global partners. Again it is a strategy of cooperation and collaboration. Lester Thurow, Professor of Management and Economics at MIT, suggests that only through full participation can we create a win/win scenario. In the recent world wide economic melt down everyone became aware of how they are connected to the global economy. Today, you are connected whether you like it or not. Your only choice is to drive or sit in the back and let someone else decide where you are going and how the journey will evolve. At Roberts we prefer the strategy of driving. In so doing we have to decide what theory will direct our driving. Where does the opportunity lie? We feel that it lies in the exporting of our production expertise and the domestic enhancement of our engineering and planning. Our advantage has always been as the source of change and improvement. This is where the future lies and the one that we want to steer toward. We want to create new jobs and opportunities for our domestic work force while creating new opportunities for our company. Cooperation and collaboration are two areas that we want to foster in our RTM for the future of Roberts.

CHAPTER TWELVE
THE PERSONAL COMMITMENT
TO TRANSFORMATION

12

*What else
do I need to
know about
transformation?*

We have spoken a lot in this book about transformation and transformational thinking. We found that transformational ideas helped us to best meet the demands of the market place. These are the ideas that come from the use of our imagination. First we imagine the future then we apply it creatively to improve our competitive position. This has helped us to create our future rather than just letting it happen. What follows is an overview, based on our experience, of why transformational methodology is so important for the creation of an effective and valuable business enterprise. The legacy approaches that follow will lead us into this discussion of innovation through imagination.

In our opinion, legacy approaches are the blocks to success and transformation is the way to overcome them. Legacy is a funny issue. Some see what has been done in the past as the journey's end. They become focused on maintaining and perhaps improving those legacy approaches. Herein lies the challenge. The fault is not with the approaches but the fact that they are seen as the end rather than just stops on the journey. What they are is new cultural equity. Here cultural equity means new sustainable value. As problems are solved, new successful approaches are created and this generates new cultural equity. We must always move forward and not get stuck accepting the present as a permanent residence. Therefore from each cultural equity stop one must continue to move forward on the Journey. Building an understanding of this fact is critical for the owner, executive or manager that wishes to keep their company from stalling out. The point is that you never arrive at the journey's end. You merely arrive at new starting points. This has been the problem with many legacy approaches in the past and has led to the failure of many a company's

Journey. So our answer is to avoid the pitfall of getting stuck with legacy approaches.

What follows are four legacy approaches that fall into this category of new starting points.

- Strategic Planning

- Total Quality Management

- Six Sigma

- Lean

Each of these approaches was created to assist organizations make progress on their transformational journey. In some cases, their popularity as approaches intersected with one another and overlapped. Let's look at them and how they have developed to fit into the new approach.

Strategic Planning was introduced to get organizations to think about their future based on the past and their current situation. The objective was to plan your way into the future with some regular activities focused on fitting better into the economic environment. What did you want to become (your vision) and what was your purpose (your mission) defined the parameters around which your plan was built. You assessed the current situation with a SWOT Analysis to point out your Strengths, Weaknesses, Opportunities and Threats. You might have used another analysis process called 7S Analysis (strategy, structure, systems, skills, staff, style and shared values) to see if all parts of your firm were properly aligned with your strategy. You then set objectives based on these analyses and action plans to achieve them. This is how it was supposed to work and how it works in most companies today. What was missing? In most cases what was missing was the development of that Pixie Dust (the thing that you are best at and is not easily replicated). It is what creates the Buffett Franchise referred to earlier in the book. 'Pixie dust' should have been the core competency element of the process all along. The development of 'Pixie dust' is what the transformational approach brings to bear. It is focused on creating the really new thing that will set an organization apart. It takes courage. There was and is nothing wrong with the strategic planning process except that it is not powerful enough on its own. It is not an end but merely a beginning that needs to be continually improved.

Total Quality Management (TQM), The National Baldrige Quality Award, Six Sigma, and Gemba all came along to assist companies improve performance. All were and have been successful. None of these were wrong but working alone each was not again powerful or broad enough to create the transformation that organizations expected. As we pointed out earlier in the book quality and on time delivery that result from these initiatives are givens. Today they are customer expectations and not something that will competitively differentiate any organization.

This is where the idea of overlaying a transformational approach on these improvement programs comes into the picture. They, or elements of them, need to be integrated and continually improved. Remember transformation is all about Pixie Dust. It creates the competitive advantage. Based on customer needs and a little imagination each organization creates its version of 'Pixie dust.' It creates a solution, or set of tools, that allows it to create a new and ever evolving customer value proposition. Once this is achieved the organization can take advantage of all of its operational excellence to deliver on a consistent manner to its customers. 'Pixie dust' is the power and it comes from a transformational mind set. Operational excellence, and the legacy ideas that support it, are only meant to play the supporting role. Never let a supporting actor play a lead role if you want your story to sell!

We hope that you will develop your own transformational model, create some 'pixie dust', and achieve a sustainable competitive advantage for yourself.

FINAL WORDS
THE CHOICE OF SUCCESS OR FAILURE

*What choices do
I have in the
approach that
I take to
transforming my
company?*

If you act without desire you will fail. What does this mean in terms of the transformational process suggested in this book? It means that if you accept the transformational ideas reluctantly, or under duress, your transformation will not be successful. If you do it only because the customer wants you to then you have placed yourself in the role of a servant. A servant does what the master wants, but reluctantly. Understand that the customer does not put you in this role. You put yourself in this role by your attitude toward the situation. If on the other hand you react with desire then the roles are ones of equals. This keeps you in charge of your half of the relationship. It makes success possible because it is what you want to have happen. The way to succeed in your transformational process is to accept with desire. This means that you have changed your mind, your relationship with your customer and your potential for success. We changed our mind, took on a new role and now understand on a different level how to succeed. We left our old competitive ideas behind and now compete by aligning our future with that of our customers. If we can help them compete we cannot help but succeed. We moved from defense to offense and this has allowed us to deliver on our brand promise to our stakeholders. We hope that you will do the same.

We hope that you have enjoyed this book and that it will help you in your endeavor to transform your organization. As stated in the book, our transformation was not a linear process. Quite to the contrary. Our process started, as many others, focused on lean. As we moved into that area, our lean consultant introduced us to the idea of cells. Embracing that idea we ran into a roadblock on how to implement it in a way that would create the end result we intended. The end result we sought was a more stable environment where we could deliver on time, meet customer quality and price objectives, and run a profitable operation on a sustainable basis. It took some time to discover that we needed to adapt a new point of view within our marketing and sales area. This new point of view, based on customer cooperation and a more collaborative process, made our transformation a success. In addition we had hired another consultant to assist us in strategy development. We focused his efforts on strategies and tactics associated with the development of our human assets. We had some success with this area but were not totally successful until we hired a new president who had a strong skill set in human assets. Looking back we would have worked on our marketing and sales strategy first. If we had spent more time in preparation I know we would have discovered this need sooner. As in sports the best way to succeed is with great preparation. In the end it all worked out but our transformational journey has not been a straight road to success.